The Caking Chronicles

Caesar Torreano

INTRODUCTION

Welcome to "The Caking Chronicles". This book tells the poetic tales of love, erotic passion, redemption but most of all, intimacy. These are some of the things that take place in an intimate encounter between lovers. It is my desire that my literary poetic tales tease your imagination and caress your heartstrings while giving you moments of clarity on the nature of love, lust and desires. I hope you enjoy every morsel of "The Caking Chronicles".

Caesar Torreano

TABLE OF CONTENTS

TABLE OF CONTENTS

THE PRELUDE

CAKE LAND

Tonight I want you to dream of cake
I want you to see me doing whatever it takes to make you fulfilled

I want you to see my arms wrapped around you as the side of your angelic
face rests upon my chest
gently snuggling to the beat of my heart.

The rain drops falling on to the grass and trees sparks the theme song to
our cake affair

Everything in me just wants you to feel so secure every place and
everywhere

Just to witness the actions of your love is so pure and
so right

As we cuddle and caress throughout the night
Enjoying our sweet moist connection
everything about you sings perfection

Indulging upon the sweet taste of our sensations
reaching all our intimate expectations

I feel joy beyond joy just in my rising anticipation
because your intimate encounters is like erotic love making without the
penetration

Our cake sessions is the greatest in all creation
It like falling madly in love with sheer desire
Your sweet batter tingles on my tongue
Its like sampling liquid fire

Coursing vigorously in my veins

Tonight I want you to feel cake
I want you to feel all my rising emotions that I carry for you

Oh how I love to slowly lick your spoon
As we spoon to destinies enchanting tune
absorbing the energy that you beautifully make
I want you to feel the passion of my kisses intake

while my hands stroke the small of your back

Sex will be just the vanilla extract for this recipe that we about to whip up
and bake

And all it takes is for you to invoke your trust in my baking skills

For I will reveal to you all the joys that your smile can bare

Just know whatever happens I will handle it with care

Tonight I want you to taste cake
I want you to taste the sweetness of my pure devotion
the devotion of a man cradling your vulnerability like a newborn
I will be your ship like anchor
keeping you grounded through any raging emotional storm

It's like tasting a blessing every time our lips touch in a passionate greeting
it's our time
it's our time my love....

The caking season

For I will only cake with you
for that loving every tier
every layer of your love is all I ever want to do

DRY INGREDIENTS
(The Pursuit)

YOU WILL.......

You're gonna remember me

Crave for me

Every tingle of your sexual palate will yearn for the taste of me
your tender thighs will open for me like Christmas morning to a child's eyes
aching for me to be between your knees

Your valley streams will heat up and run over past passions limited degrees
Your hunger, that hungers to beat down your walls, I will feed oh so
generously

I will destroy your lustful inhibitions completely
make the tips of your areola lump; goose bump and tighten up for my
tongue briskly
Make your O's rise and climb heavenly

As I push between your pelvis with pure potent pipe
While teasing your ta-tas oh so gently
Filling your feminine flower with my climbing essence from threshing in
the threshold of ecstasy

Then comforting you with my caking comfort as your fragile frame resides
next to me

I'm gonna make your desires haunt you to be physically haunted by me

And all you have to do for me.............

is give in to the seduction of desire

TEASING ME IN RHYTHM

Erotically she dances for me slowly
impressively her visual foreplay sweetly entices me

Her eyes invite me to caress her lips
as she whines her finger tips on the wetness of her cavity

But in actuality……..
I never wanted anyone this much in my whole life
strife from craving her is what's teasing and taunting within me

Daydreaming about making her cream and it's not a reality
her teasing memory evokes in me a thirst that goes unquenched

A honey hole that I'm dying to patrol
feeding every inch of my shaft with swift rolls

Those bedroom eyes have me tantalized
driving my erection past the point of fracture
igniting a fire that's set to explode
to her I want to unfold my inner freak
I yearn for the sugar rush of her sweet juicy peach
until I fall into the grips of a coma like sleep

She makes my will weak
as she glides her hands inside the inner part of her thighs

Swaying her hips staring at me
displaying to me her resume on how she can ride
rubbing her forbidden spot
like she's burning hot, dying for me to make her climatically climb

Her aura is singing, "sex me"
I can't keep my feelings refined
I will always lust for her captivating frame
at least until the end of my time

For she is fine wrapped in the sexiness of beauty
sensuality captures her personality along with the pursuing naughtiness of
her sexual advances

I was down
sprung, strung out and spellbound
when I first met her glance

As she slow rocked to soothing seductive rhythms
smiling at me as she erotically danced

Teasing my intimate lustful thoughts
dying to have that chance
to know the taste of her sweet rhythm

THE CRUSH

I see your sexy from afar
I gaze into your alluring eyes as an astrologer gazes upon illuminating stars

For I desire for you to be my star
In my erotic episodes

For tonight you are my Da Vinci Code
and my producing cunnilingus is my decipher
to all your decoded secrets
to what makes you climb higher and higher
for in my active imagination you are the master of all my self happy endings

The reflection of your sexy frame just keeps bending
and bending my very fabric of all my intimate desires

For when I dream about you
I dream about fire engulfed in passion
I dream about serving you sexually in a glorious fashion
I think about your inferno blazing me sweetly to burn
I imagine being deep in your creamy box
and all I can do is joyfully churn
as I joyfully jack knife you with your toes in my mouth

Let me be the ambassador to your wetness
as my tongue travels to your tight south
I breathe my lust for you in and out

For there is no doubt
for I have a crush on crushing you through and through.

Because all I want to do..........
is do you
not just in my imagination or dreams

DREAM WOMAN

I know love

The addiction of it

To love a person with every angle of your being
because the only way I know to love is hard

The only way I know to adore a woman is completely
the only way I know how to hold up women is to the heavens.

When it comes to loving a Lady
I perform it like painting a work of art
with light brushes of color and life encased in a beautiful frame as you are.
Choose me, my love, as I long to make you mine.
Hold me captive with your passion
allow me to be entwined in the ecstasy of your heart, your soul, and your
sex
Just thinking about it makes me a little scared

But I could never fear adoring and treasuring you my treasure
The world should nickname you my Bling
Give me a monument of you and I'll give you my everything that I
physically and emotionally own
There's no boundaries; no limits to being loved by something almost
perfect.
I stand corrected
because I don't see a flaw in you my love
to be absorbed in a utopia of bliss
wrapped in mortal flesh

Possessing immortal love that can't be defined in our lifetime
I love you with my heart
I love you with my soul
I love you with my everything
The keeper of my peace and the author of my happy ever after
I don't want to dream you no more
I want you to be within my reality
I want you out the back of my sub-conscious cerebral and in my surreal
lined up in my peripheral
I want to feel the warmth of your skin and the kiss of your lips and not
worry about waking up

I want you to exist as the love for you exists in my heart.
Right when I'm about to cave into the belief that there not a right one for me
The Déjà Vu of your dreamscape keeps my hopes alive.

 I desire to hold your hand, and stand next to your presences in real time,
not in dream time
until I fall asleep
without waking up alone.

TRADING PLACES

Hello Ms Monogamous
You are beautiful through and through

Please indulge me for a moment
Please may I ask you

How does your boo feel to be the luckiest man on the planet earth
To possess an Angelic creature whose beauty flows like a perfect poetic
verse
Like when Maya Angelou genius-ly gave birth to her first stanza of
Phenomenon Woman
Ask him for me.......

How does it feel to make love to the answer of the question of where
heaven resides

To, taste and embrace a utopia of excellence every time you spread
passionately eagle wide
To carry the joy inside of having a person of pure greatness

If you were mine every night
I would joyfully cry to Jehovah for your presence
Your essence glazes my senses in crisp completeness

And Baby you don't even belong to me
Ask your man what does he see when you're residing in the grasp of his
mere mortal arms
as you intuitively bless his being with your celestial like charms
Tilling away his cares away while leaving his heart unharmed

I would be up in arms to let you out the line of my sight
nonetheless have any man likes me within your line of sight
For I know any red blooded man would lustfully yearn for you
and that your smile would drive any man's senses wild
making his nature bloom like a rose to sunlight

You will make his desires soar like a sparrow in flight
he will ache for the essence of you
like a nocturnal creature aches for the interior of the night

I would just about give away everything in my life

to trade places with him so you could be my everything......
My wife

For you are a treasure, my love
To be appraised priceless; like a rare find
For you as a whole blow my mind

So I want to ask you this just one more time

How does your man feel to have someone as great as you?

INTIMATE GAMES

I promise you this, my love: one roll of the dice and I'll make you mines
I'm Sorry you had to go three steps back

But please step up because we don't have much time
Know that I will never cheat on you for I know that you are a fair game.

I want to process and caress your Chess game as your pawn slide towards
my bishop.
Your touch gently caresses my dice in your hands

So let me ask you
Are you ready for my Monopoly of pleasure?
I invited you to my hotel room at Park Place
 With much haste hoping that your thimble lands upon me.
Slowly tonguing and fondling your 25,000 Pyramid of play
for I promise I won't be the Weakest Link in this session of ours

Your Tic Tac Toe foreplay is no match for mines
For I will make you block out all your X's with me giving you multiple O's
vertically and horizontally across your board
Let our Family Feud for I claim you tonight as my sexual lifeline

Deal or No Deal
If the Price Is Right I will gamble anything to have one roll of the dice
To hit seven eleven on your table and don't worry I won't crap out early
my gingerbread man has entered your Candy Land
 Strolling and stroking down your sticky narrow pathway,
 As ours emotions and bodily fluids get Scrambled in the process
Calling and hitting on all your numbers until you're screaming Bingo
Pokeeno and Yahtzee

Who's your daddy
you don't need to go to the Maury show to find that shit out

You see I gave you Clues to all the ways I wanted to play you

until you know that I'm Uno when it comes to making you cum in this sex
game
And that I'm the one with an active tongue that aches to lick up and down
your Shoots and Ladders

And I will go faster until I Bongo your entire world
oh how I love your head games you give good brain like a surgical genius

Taking me to the point of ecstasy putting me in Jeopardy of never wanting
another woman again.
Simon said don't stop grinding with me until we reach the heavens in a
Sutter of climactic pleasure

Explosions that I'm sure that will shake cloud nine to its foundation

Oh how I love to Operate on you
touching and playing with your pleasure bone until you go off

I won't stop lying, loving and playing you because Baby you
are the best game I ever played.

IMAGINATION INVASION

Can I navigate and motivate your imagination?
Can I touch you and tease you to the point of cremations?
Can I ride and grind you
leaving your climatic limitations in utter devastation?
For that you are my greatest inspiration when my sexual desires are called
on deck.
For I will gain from you sexual respect when I redefine for you the meaning
of an afterglow.
For I will evoke every dirty thought I know to make you surrender your
imagination to me.
For after I use my erotic techniques
that will charge that inner freak so it can run free.
Can I navigate and motivate your imagination?
May I embrace you with my swift thrusts that will change forever how you
lust and bust on penetration?
Your moans and screams of delight I will forever expand, increase,
and alter.
My legacy will feel so sweet to you that you will call me the other name that
you call your father
No need to try to ever bother with ever trying to replace another for me
because these lustful thoughts will make the greatest of the great piper's halt
when they hear all the naughty and nasty things that I plan to do to you my
love.
Can I navigate and motivate your imagination until you experience a sweet
warm sensation that gives you a sweet tingle between your legs.
For the richness and the width of my manhood, my love, you will never
ever have to beg.
For I desire from you a taste test
followed by a lustful stroke fest
for it will make you confess how good my night stick stimulates you
with a passionate purpose of pleasing you as I beat it up
Because I desire to make you smile beyond the barriers of your nature smile
while I'm rigorously stirring it up.
Because I will continue to assault
all your most intimate thoughts until I make you all mine.
Can I navigate and motivate your imagination................................

PATIENTLY

I will wait for your wet grace
Patiently I shall hold off for your taste
For you to place me in your intimate trust
To be permitted to ravage upon you my aching lust
To be privileged to be between your fragile frame, licking, and delivering to
you passionate thrusts
I don't mind waiting up because good things come to those who wait
But when it's our time I won't hesitate to break you off
To suckle on all your hills and valley in and out right lustful assault
Nothing will make me halt until we reach our destination....... cloud nine
Enjoying our physical journey in erotic touching and feverish hungry
grinds
As our lips entwined on each others lips become intoxicated by one another
like fine wine
So I don't mind taking my time
For I will be patient for you
I will even hold my breath for you
For when you're with me, my love, you give me air
Anything broken in my life, your presence can easily repair
To rush being with you and then miss you would be more than I could
ever bear
For I was addicted to your nature when I was caught up in your glare
For when you make your path to me I know that I must prepare... ......
To bare sweet satisfaction beyond anyone can ever compare
So I will wait and prepare to be turned out and happy

WET COMPONENTS
(The Sexual Encounters)

TONIGHT

Tonight let your wetness be the witness to our secret
The secret to how to reach the heavens without dying
To soar among hills and valleys without use of flying
When your seductive wet twilight is brushing upon my lips, it is so inviting
We reach new plateaus when I lick you from head to toe
 For it is my midnight hunger that you delight in
To tongue your labia creases in slight pieces under the pale moonlight
To fill your aching wet void with my hardened hammer
Passionately beating it up throughout the night
The gateway into your volcanic layer always stays so hot and tight
Spilling your hot magma among my tense territories
Let me sacrifice my explosive seeds in your layer in the midst of a climactic
glory
As I make your orgasms climb ten stories; feeding you my thick pleasures
with no light in sight
I want you to grab me by my mane as I hold your vessel ever so tight
As I deliver to you parades of stroke
For with you I yearn to lie
Serving to you just right
All night with my nocturnal sex play
Get wicked for you in the witching hour
Not stopping until our desires break for day
For we indulge in our afterhours ride
Serving each other sexual lullabies until our desires give way
My insomnia will be in full effect
For tonight I elect to stay up in you all night long

DAMN.............

Damn.............
My senses are tingling
my inward lust is fiending for the residue of you
my manhood rises with anticipation
Throbbing......
Aching ....
Hungering to bend your body for it is ecstasy that is awaiting
as I make you dripping wet from your tight va-jay
for tonight my bedroom shall suffice as our own personal cirque du soleil
Obsessive memories of you striding me
being ever so freaky
as my night shaft churns into you with full force ever so vigorously
Until your cream streams to the top
For I want to make your O's run nonstop
Until hours and hours have ran past the clock
Until the rhythms in your heartbeat threaten to flutter and stop
Until all your wetness drops
Making my mattress a kiddie pool
Damn can I be for you.......?
Can I be your pipelaying fool
Let my tongue lick sweet something in your under carriage
Have your labia feeling so blissful until it makes proposals to my lips of
marriage
For tonight I vow to be your fairest stroke of your sexual all
Penetrate in your perfect place
Have your peaks climbing a hundred feet tall
damn I want your all......
I want your all tonight
Damn I want to feel every crease and angles of your wet delights
I want you to speak into my hardened Mic and spit for me a hundred
lapping bars
Can I get in my car
Damn Baby please......
can I get in my car.......
And run it on you fast like an Olympic track star
can I come to you
And make you cum for me
As you bring my desires out the shadows of its hungering depths
Damn......
These desires of mines won't be moved
So please can I give all of me.....
To the all of you

AN ORAL EROTIC TALE

He approached her
He kissed her lips
As his fingertips slightly danced upon her wet tight place
with no haste he sought to give attention to her lower waist
to her cave of sweet wonders he applied his face
she moaned loudly as he glazed his tongue in her throbbing wet place
as her sweet cream streamed down his visage, unto his trembling lips.
The message that his cunnilingus whispered to her lips
spoke sweet secrets sealed in licks and gentle kisses
She pulls his head close to her aching bliss
while she levees an ocean in his suckling mouth.
He enjoyed the taste of her climactic
Bout as her wet essence glazed around his cheeks and chin
as her legs shake vigorously from her va-jay being ascended to heaven's lair
As he lapped voraciously all in
as his lustful hunger serviced all her delights with his mighty thick tongue
He was sprung on being her conduit to oral intimacy
Spellbound completely by her orgasmic nectar
Having a jolly good, enjoyable time
she joyfully whined as he dined on her feverishly
As she was spread eagle wide from behind.
And she orgasmic-ly climbed
and climbed
Until he clocked the height of her O's as the Himalaya Mountains
her screaming, and shouting,
As her juicy peach runneth over like a fountain,
From being mixed ecstasy elixir was his own enriched reward
His tireless tongue soared,
While he played Marco Polo through both of her portals of her please-ment
Invoking upon her sheer pleasure
and she got wetter, and wetter
As his lips sailed through her juices with his neck sufficing as an anchor.
For him it got no better than to indulge in the moistness of her tender
buffet
for on this day he was dedicated to pleasing her without penetration
sexing her from a selfless act
to give her selfish pleasure

ALPHABETIC EROTICA

A   is for my **Appetite** that surges when I am gazing upon you.

B   is for the shortened **Breaths** I take when I imagine you on top of me.

C   is for the **Cunnilingus** that I vow to perform on you feverishly.

D   is for how **Deep** I desire to go in you, as deep as the raging sea.

E   is the **Ecstasy** I experience when I am engulfed in your sexual grasp.

F   is for the **Flavor** of your sweet flesh that I indulge in from your neck, down to your sweet ass.

G   is for your **G spot** that I plan to target all damn day.

H   is for the **Heavens** that I see when our physical actions are in play.

I   is for you **Immortalizing** me when I am locked in the chambers of your physical thrust.

J   is for this delightful **Journey** that I explore inside you that I just can't get enough.

K   is for the **Kindred** spirits that we are, when we share the art of our lovemaking.

L   is how you **Lay** with me after our erotic play has been taken.

M   is for the **Mere** **Mortal** in me that has been blessed to have sampled a goddess.

N   is for the **Nectar** of your sweet flesh, for that I would have joyfully traveled the farthest.

O   is the **Organism** eruptions that I will give you as we play into this erotica script.

P   is the **Perfection** I experience from the taste and embrace of all four of your lips.

Q   is for the **Quality** that I enjoy in your captivating stimulating touch.

R   is for the **Radiance** that I feel; to others it seems to be too much.

S   is for the **Simplicity** that I feel when it comes to adoring you.

T   is for the **Tenderness** that I feel at night when I'm caressing and holding you.

U   is for the **Utopia** I feel when I am between the eclipses of your tender thighs.

V   is for **Venus** I see in your universe causing my mercury to rise.

W   is for your **Walls** that my manhood scales like a blind man scrolling braile.

X   is for how I beat it up like a **Xylophone,** which you inclined for me to beat it up well.

Y   is for how I **Yearn** for the wetness of you and all the intangible pleasures that you bring.

Z   is for the **Zulu** which you bring out in me; for that you make me feel like the worlds original king.

My desire can run from **A to Z** because of the physical presence that you bring.

That's why you make my alphabets sing ...... how much I want you.

THE INFILTRATION

Let my lust in
or I will huff and I will puff and lick your labia walls down
Take your climaxes to its breaking
 limits as my cunnilingus polishes your vaginal crown
Out flank your inhibition restraints
spinning your nature completely all around
The art of war and sexual play for me walks hand in hand
Strategically setting off my lustful assaults
 so we can get off is all a part of my desiring plan
I will caress your fragile frame with my hands
as my lips scan and glaze your tender skin
As I feel your frigid barrier
located in your forbidden area starting to cave in
Your body is committing treason
screaming for only one reason……
to let me in
I will bend the very fabric of the sensual in your sensuality
probing the deepest depths of all your fantasy aspects evoking it into reality
And all you have to do is…….
let me in
And this epic erotic warfare will begin
with my lips to your breast
Tongue to your spur
and my hardening shaft will handle the rest
My pleasurable techniques
will make your valley peak and confess
Let my infiltration gratify our love making
Until your earth starts shaking from orgasms by me
As I invade you blissfully
dropping bombs over your Baghdad
I'm not your Dad but you will label me Poppi for that I would bring true
sexual satisfaction in your inhibited world
For your freaky-ness to me is as mature as the average girl but my freak will
make it peak to womanhood
My invasion to you will feel so, so good
if you allow my third leg-acy to march in
For the creaminess of your wetness I will forever battle for and contend
Let my lust in or I will huff….
and I will puff…..
and lick your labia walls down

MRS. HYDE

Mrs. Hyde is who I desire to see tonight
I request the intimately confident
sexually dominate
Grab me by my hair
Willing to get it in anywhere
Openly honest alter sexual ego of yours
I have your transformation elixir on standby….
A few shots of 1800 Gold that should bring that freak to the surface
Dirty flicks, tongue tricks
followed by firm slaps on her ass is all on the resume of how she likes to
get off
Nothing is ever off limits in the event of being inside the wet Mrs. Hyde
The request of hot wax
and jackknifing her on her back is just the beginning on her list of erotica
And me placing my lips on every hole that she possesses
playing her desires like a fucking harmonica
I want the freak who loves to be ridden hard and put away wet
Putting every single lustful thought she has in effect to give us pleasure
But Mrs. Hyde, Mrs. Hyde I know what really gets your goat
A hard slow grind on the wall engulfed in an intimate hard wind
while my hand is slightly laced across your throat
And as I increase the torque of my banging thrust
Going faster with you in sensual sequence
As you scream to me "harder I'm about to bust"
To me your primal nature is second to none
Especially when you're riding me
in the thaws of ecstasy biting on my shoulders when you're about to cum
riding
Leaving your mark on me that you were here and that you rocked my world
Mrs. Hyde loves to call me nasty mutha fuckas when I'm hitting her
switches in full control
No hold or hole on her body is out of bounds when she's in the drivers seat
And her favorite slogan that she orally live by
that when she physically repeats it makes my toes curl
"Spitters are quitters"
And I remember that time when she made me bust back to back
Because her head game was genius that night
when she had Caesar on her pleasure rack

So many pleasures that I can't even measure
because of her methods that she use in our sexual bouts
For that hidden part
That freaky part in every part
always leaves me....
lost and turned out

HER PERFECT STORM

I know where my physical heaven lies
Its lies in the moist clouds between her sweet thighs
Each layer increase
that strikes in me a thunderous release
that can't be put into mere words.
It's like we defy all laws of physics
when we get explicit in executing our lustful actions that surge.
Feeling the calm before her violent beautiful storm
Anticipating lustful thoughts
and everything that turns hers on
Tracing around her areolas is like sampling cotton candy while floating in
the midst of clouds
her hurricane approaches
the sweet scent of moisture in the air drives my senses wild
Slowly I caress my tongue upon her flesh
Feasting upon her breast and spur performing for her my own rain dance
Making her wetness enhance
so nectar rain can drench my chin
and then she goes all in
With her hurricane fellatio that made me bust and let go my future family
tree
And then she touched down on me
Riding me like a twister in the midst of March
Tearing apart my will of not being blown away by her sexual techniques
My inner freak forecasts for me
a night of hot wet sensations
and blissful penetrations
that will be grinding in the eye of her organismic storm
The memories of her erotic wetland falls turn me on
and when it's in full swarming effect turning me out.
There is no doubt that being caught up in her tropical
is the best thing that happened to me.
For that she is to me…..
My perfect storm.

THE KAT BURGLAR

Lustful larceny is what stalks my appetite
Embezzling the sweetness of your fit will give me such delight
Slowly my lips tip toe down to your labia space
My cunnilingus is using licking combinations
to open up your creamy flood gates
I'm a clitoris klepto, looking to steal all your O's
To physically taste and penetrate every passage that pleases you is my only goal
To lap the pinkness of your panther is the answer to how do I love to get off
You turn my shaft to hard from soft when I'm gazing upon the treasures of your chest
To grind and make you climactically climb
 with my width is a crime of passion I'm willingly to confess
Under your dress will be my point of infiltration
Creasing your heated cavity with the fingers of my tips unlocking all your cremations
Anticipation teases me when thinking about the grind-mation to your private of pearls
Cracking your safe
as I rotate my waist makes your pitch of passion
high as a little girl
The temptations of your tight box haunt my thoughts twenty-four seven
Ready to set it off
with a lustful assault,
so I can coast in your oceans of eleven
Heaven is what I will evoke in you from the blissfulness of my crimes
Cumming through your front and behind your door,
as you scream "give it to me more and more"
Polishing you with my family jewels
as our desires for one another rule
while we roll around on the floor
Your climax alarm triggers off
as the control from your left leg not to shake off aborts
Your eyes are so relaxed and so soft
from my legacy scaling your walls
and kicking down your doors
The evidence of my erotic caper is laced across my waist
and deep within in my chin pours
For that I will always sinfully adore
 shoplifting the tightness of you

COMMAND

Your sexual will belongs to me tonight
An even keel of pleasurable wonders is what you will receive outright
The addiction of my dictatorship
Will whip your wetness like waters from a tide
As I drop anchor on your floor bed as my strokes cums in wide
I command you......
To tease the tips of your breast across my lips
While my hands grip your hips as your moistness starts brewing down south
Slowly I will swirl them in my mouth simultaneously making my tongue flick
Then my licks will stream to your heavenly split
Perform rapid lapping techniques on your vaginal lips and your clit
I demand you to evoke your inner fiend
That Jones' for my Johnson to sex Ms. Kitty vigorously
Who aches for my legacy to inherit her physically
So just obey me tonight
And I promise like I done before to make you see the lights of heaven
without leaving the borders of my bedroom
Your erotica have my hardened shaft in full mushroom bloom and its harvest time
Everything of yours that can satisfy me sexually I claim as mines
For you are my spoil of war
All your climax limitations I plan to destroy
As you grind with me hastily with tears of joy tracing the lids of your eyes
As my lips brush yours while I go deep in your insides
Flipping upon you all my freakiest tricks
That order your body to climb at my will
For that you will......surrender all to this erotic episode
No holds will be barred while I'm inches deep up to your appetite
For on this night I command your all unto me

HER VINEYARD

You are my fine wine
I enjoy partaking in a sip from your glass
the acidity of your passions tingle my tasteful glances

While your alluring exquisite flavor blesses my mouth in a thirst quenching
dance
A taste that tantalizes my taste buds;
 wishing forever for it to longingly last
As my unhinged desire for you flows and grows every time I swallow your
intoxicating mass

Joyfully indulging your great vintage
Our erotic binging scrimmages blaze me like a perfectly aged merlot
Its sweet nectar quickens me blissfully as I slowly drink of you from head to
toe

You sample so smooth and sweet like a chilled flute of Moscato
Drinking in the moments of our passion until reaching the end of your
blissful bottle

Your vineyard applies so flawlessly to my hungering soul
You are a descendant of greatness
for it is your potent elixir I ache to consume whole

My thirst for your communion knows no limits
For it is you that I yearn to consume until finish

For my thirst for my passion will not diminish till I'm under the influence
of your nectar
For it is your exquisite favor that elevates me
and stimulates me
to higher sectors of tipsy physical bliss

My thirsting desires, oh so enjoy this......
Drink the pure essence of you
Through Erotica's glass
toasting to your supreme excellence

THE BLEND
**(The Combination of Infatuation
& Physical Availabilities)**

WHEN I WAKE UP

My morning is always good when I awake next to you
My morning mental is always in a better mood
when we find consciousness in each others' arms
When the sun's rays reflects off your face
even through glimpse eyes I am just charmed
Thanking God within that He allowed one of His celestial beings to lay next
to me
blessing me so beautifully in the genesis of my day
The blend of fresh hazelnut coffee along with your tender kisses takes my
breath away
Effortlessly awakens me out the sandman's trance
The sound of your voice along with sparrows singing
makes my soul within yearn to dance
It's like an early bird romance
As I bid you good morning
stroking your visage
leaning in to steal from you another kiss
Our breakfast intimacy enlist that we share
is my wake up call to bliss
when I'm in my deep subconscious slumber
Just to know it is within my arms that you are resting under
Guarantees for me sweet dreams
I don't ever want to have to wonder
How it feels at the beginning of my day
without your presence
Good Morning
                    My Love

SENSUAL LOC'S IN

She stares at my mane
as her lustful appetite starts to extend
She caresses my loc's as our lips
lock letting our desires gives in
She yearns within for them to be draped across the small of her torso
As I take my time indulging in the fine sweetness of her creamy wet morsel
In her hand she winds them tight
as I deliver to her passionate steady grinds
But when I'm behind, my loc's become her sexual best friend
Pulling me closer and closer
as we get our playtime in
A sweet sin that infringes on her to react passionately
Making her cum crazy
until she's on the brink of her sexually insanity
She says to me that I'm her Samson
for no other can ever compare
Because of the strength of my freakiness resides in my hair
for with her I'm eagerly willing to share
But my strength doesn't just lie there
It thrives in what I lust and what I know
I've been a freak for my whole forever
but my vanity is just something to grab a hold
A safety belt that you can console
when my ride of epic-ness makes her tremble and shake
When my tongue plays in her all day
making her climaxes desperate for a break
Aggressively she reels me in
wrapped in a odyssey of ecstasy and all its enchanting blends
Then our erotic escapade descends
stripping our mortal souls bare
My soft loc's are laced across her face
as our sweet scent is still in the air as we wake
For me to be a part of her sexual intakes
Makes me with no debate
Happy to be nappy

WHEN YOU'RE IN MY ARMS

When you are in my arms I feel tranquility and serenity all in one embrace
Just the taste of your beauty gives such gentle calm to my raging beast
The release that I feel intoxicates me
as we kill time adoring one another
In your arms within me I feel no pain
I have no strain about the world or about being vulnerable with my
emotions or heart
You lying in my arms sparks the feeling that you will love me for who I am
When your visage rests upon my chest my life doesn't seem so damned
When engulfed in the rapture of your love I finally know who I am
I am an original King like out of a dream
when you're within my grasp
A feeling forever and ever that I wish will lingeringly last
I am the happiest man on the third planet from the sun
Our past troubles, pains and strains are suddenly undone
Regret has no bearing when our intimacy is engaged
As we are in our euphoric paradise
 enjoying our satisfied selves
When she's in my embrace she says I am the best version of a teddy bear
she ever felt
The warmth that generates while she lay under my bicep soothes her to
beautiful dreams
As I have sweet dreams that she will never let me go
No women will ever uphold…..
the high that I feel while you're in my arms.

PLEASURES OF HER UTOPIA

I feel the grippingness of her erotic memory
The taste that your labia embraces upon me that is addicting my senses
Splendid is what comes to me as I cum with you in ecstasy
Legendary is the fleet that I feel after releasing in you my legacy
Your sweet walls press me to unexplainable pleasures
I feel the Elysian Fields in your grinds
your pressure gets better and better
The gateway to your heaven gets wetter and wetter
as your climactic of angels appears
Our lips are quickly caressing one another
as the sound of your peaking rapture blesses my ears
The sweetness of your fit has at times brought me to tears
It is you, who I sexually revere,
for our lustful encounters satisfy me in full
I've been a teacher for a while in pipe-ology
but when you're on top of me you take me to school
Your seductive devices that heat up like spices turn my desires inside out
I ache for the essence of your epic-ness
for that I have no doubts
For at times I fear that my body will never commandeer a miracle like you
ever again
For that it will be a bitter end
for me to not again sample the blissfulness of your box
Your rhythmic rotations
along with your oral sensation have my sexual tendencies on lock
Joyfully I go down to bathe in the hot of your honey pot that massages
upon my lips
Feeling the pressure of you reeling me in as you slow wind with the rhythm
of your hips
I see the eclipse of your moon rising as my tongue swims against your
raging tide
To witness the breaking of your heated levees fills my oral techniques with
such pride
For that I have licked the heavens and found perfection
 when I fell in love with the inside of your utopia

BREATHLESS

You take my breath away
Every day when I witness the love you show for me
Indeed you are my solider that goes to battle for me day in and day out
I can't control my inhales or exhales
because you possess the true origins of its patterns
I will always revolve around the essence of your love above
as the rings that orbits around its Saturn
Your emotion
your heart
your wind ascends me parasailing my soul to the heavens
No oxygen, dioxide or pride will ever keep me from indulging your love
That's so elegantly floating within me
The essence of my life is glazed with your light
and imprints your influences upon my existence
That's why I will always stand for you love and fight for you for this I will
be very persistent
Let your wind carry us away to a land beyond a land
Where breathing is optional and loving each other is mandatory
Where intimacy, serenity ranges higher than ten stories
Where love is shown from true raw emotions sequenced in action
Combined with blissful satisfactions
along with desires and devotion that read in every action like an enchanted
love novel
It would not be a problem for me to be with you until life leaves me
Until your air, our love exhales from our vessels
so to you I will make this decree
I would rather settle to be with you for one day and then fade away
than to go on living without you my beloved
For I will devotedly follow wherever your beautiful breeze takes me
nothing will ever be above it
For you to shed one tear to me in pain, to me it's an unforgiveable sin
Because your joy beyond joy that I eagerly employ
sends me back to where my true happiness begins
Because no matter what others may think
or what others may say
I know that your divinity that captivates me completely
will always take my breath away
In every waking hour and in every waking day
Your love and your beauty that always weakens me
will forever take my breath away
Leaving me breathless!

MY TECHNIQUE

My technique is so sweet,
Flawless through and through
A poster child for excellence when it comes to adoring you
Our desires were perfectly designed to solely cater and pleasure one another
For you I'll be more than a lover
Your orgasmic conduit when we are under the covers
I know every inch of you my love
Even down to where your toes divide
Even the spots that make you piping hot
to the point where it make you passionately cry
My technique is so, so sweet
When I'm holding and adoring you
My effect sometimes
makes you intimately climb just by consoling the presence of you
For you bring out the flawlessness in me
constancy keeps me in the zone
Knowing everything that lustfully applies to you
Your senses and desires I own
Let me cook for you my love
Meatloaf, salad, and creamy mash on the side
a couple of chilled glasses of Merlot
followed up by a long passionate heated ride
I'll taste your sweet honey for hours
and I vow I won't take a break
I'll give you multiple after multiple climbs
until your left leg aches from all its shakes
And after we finish taking our physical journey
that I know will leave us tired and weak
I'll do the Drake and say to you "you're the best"
As I rub the small of your back until you fall asleep.
My technique only surfaces when I'm around someone loving and true
To some it may seem flawed
but it's perfectly designed for you.

PRIVILEGED

Blessed be me
For I felt the moistness of your hot rapture internally
it was so magnificent to me
With the way our throbs matched each pulse perfectly
our climactic climb rocked us intuitively
Amplifying my desires completely
Your lustful waves tsunami me
overwhelming my line of sight
Only to gaze upon our erotic appetite
Your sexual nature has become my light
We unite in these steamy sexual unions
Ravaging one another's mortal vessels while our souls are consuming
perfection

Letting passion be our teacher showing us the direction to heaven on earth
My desire had an unquenchable thirst
Until I embraced your wet utopia
residing under your skirt

That fits perfectly just for me
That capsize my passionate cravings
that overwhelms me beautifully

Blessed be me
That your wetness knows the surface of me
For I'm so privileged to have indulged your wet all
That soothes my senses from you…..
giving me your all

THE ART

The art of love making is a mural
An image
A portrait for the heart that never lies
A feast for the emotional soul
It will make you flourish and thrive
That will take you to unexplainable highs
while sweetly blazing your essence
To bask in its true effervescence will tantalize your vessel as a whole
more than just physical
Much more than incredible
With its every touch, its entry can flow you to Agapes bond
For it will make two existences bond
when their desires beautifully whine in an erotic dance
Letting your artistic ecstasy prance
on the canvas of your bedroom sheets
It will have you embracing heaven's glance
that views to the human eye so sweet
As your body dry runs to heaven's gates
The commitment of your auras, to one another
For its allegiance it can ever be undone
Its stroking rhythms can become your air
and illuminate your life like the sun
It's climaxes can blissfully be your moon
A climaxing tide that can ripple through your emotional barriers and being
like a raging typhoon
Chanting anticipation
that layers upon your layers a soothing sensation
willing beautiful reasons to your emotional rhyme
An elevated plateau that can't be defined
With crisp completeness its afterglows will satisfy you so smooth
The beautifulness painting in the room........
That's what the art of love making is to me

THE BAKING
(The Caking of Intimacy and Emotions)

OUR MOMENTS

We are faithful to our moments
Where our cares are stripped bare
and our desires seek atonement
All our urges and passionate intents
our mortal vessel absorbs it
The caking sessions that we feverishly set
your angelic nature is always in enrollment
As our kisses dances with sweet destiny
and the love we share feels like heaven on earth
For you are my perfect verses
 in the scroll of true Agape
You are my everything to me my love
That brings out the best in me
For I vow
To be for you your all........
and I swear to keep your happiness in full awe
when I relate to you
I thank God's fate for entwining me and you
For you have pure perfection gracefully lying deep in the wilderness of you
That's why I will always be faithful to you
And the moments that our love shares

CATER TO YOU

Let tonight be an outright catering session for your mind, body and soul
I wanna make every angle of you to feel physically and mentally privileged
from the top of your head to the bottom of your toes
Let me apply a stimulating caressing flow to all your limbs while you vent
about your work day
Let me untense your untenseable
mold you into a flawless mood like potters molds perfect rations of clay
Prepare you a gourmet meal that teases the tips of your palette in a blissful
way
Lemon ice cream for dessert
covered in cooked cherries from a rum based flambé
Draw you a hot bubble bath in the twilight
with fresh rose petals on top for display
Scented candles illuminate the path to your soaking session
With a flute of Moscato as a chaser to chase all cares away
Then I'll serenade your ears with sweet poetic soliloquies
while it blends in the background blissfully with tracks of Marvin Gaye
Then quiet storm you will blame until manana
Until the moon fades for the break of day
For you are my everything
My source of strength in my everyday
So tonight I vow to prove it to you
In every form
In every sense
And in every way
By catering to a Queen........
By catering to you

REMINISCENT OF PASSION

On this warm night I feel loved
gazing at the late night stars thinking of you

Enjoying my enlisting times in my mental mind
to relive that night through and through

For it was so warm that evening when our desires physically pursued

Even hotter was your heavenly passage as my hardened rapture joyfully
within you moved

Our aching pleasure grew along with the moisture from our sweat

Oh how I love your honey to glaze me
your grinding rhythms tying to me so perfect

That why I elect to fantasize about the greatness of that night we shared

When I put aside my cares
and ravished your nakedness bare

The twilight of our appetites was not prepared for our intimate creativity

Or my hungering ability to sample upon you all night long

That's why the memory of our episode replays to me so so strong....

the night of our passion

SHE SAYS

She said that I'm the man of her dreams
manifested in her physical reality
A shining black knight
that brings blissfulness to her morning, noon and nights
A supreme lover fulfilling all her awaited fantasies
She says my amore makes her entire body soar
defying all the laws of gravity
She says it's not just causality
that our loving endearments mimic each other so accurately
She says my voice sounds the sound of her true divinity
taking her cares away completely
soothing her lunging soul to solace
While I drink upon the sweet elixir from her chalice
For it is her kindness that wills me peace
For she is my perfect peace when my soul seeks the sanctuary of slumber
Her touch defines the true meaning of radiance
The sensual sunlight in my greatest springs and summers
For my heart she swears to never leave it asunder
She is the sweet cream at the end of my hard ice
Our intimacy blends so richly, so nice
Deeming our love making the perfect sundae
For she yearns each day
For the feel of my warm caress Monday through Sunday
To be able to indulge upon the presence of me
As I hunger for the moist secretions flowing from her beautiful bounty
All she wants me to be.......
here only to love her
support her
patiently nurture her
and to be quickened upon the aura of her exclusively
She says I can be the foundation of our greatness
if I trust her to be my earth
And from the richness of her soil a prism of pure loyalty can be given birth
A paradise where we're immune from past pain, strain and insufferable hurt
But before it's all said and done
For what it's all truly worth.........
she is the everything that I've wished for
That's why we say..........
we are made for each other

INTIMATE RELAXATION

Relax your mind
Put the irrelevance of the world's cares far behind your mind
Allow yourself the opportunity to be adored
to be physically praised through your every pore
Indulge in your inward amore
accept the sweetness of solace
that I will have plentifully in store for you my love
Let me offer you my expanded hands
to perform upon your calves and feet a delightful relaxing dance
Massaging all your pleasant nerve endings
until you are locked in a sedated like trance
allow that chilled glass of Moscato to linger upon your tasteful glands
and while you're on your sipping game
I will patiently stand behind you
caressing your shoulders with my healing hands
while allowing me to be your venting tool
Our laws of where our intimacy rules
don't always consist of me physically penetrating you
Let me mentally wind with you
Let my caking dine with you
indulge upon all of its moist parts
Lay your back to the front of my chest and become in tune with the beats
of my heart
That in rhythm-atic drum rolls to your presence
As we possess each other is essence
Embracing the effervescence of tranquility's great lessons
Allow this soothing moment to make your being feel so magnificent
While serenity has your cerebral in its grasp
Let your troubles not be steadfast
Let our vexes not be relevant
Let all the ill wills be a distant memory of your past
But intake the elegance of my cake
So just take..........
Your cares off for me
And let peace cease the moment
For I will never cease....
 bringing peace to you!

IT IS HER

Her breast and her eyes
Her torso that leads to her thighs
I'm mesmerized by where her beauty lies
It lies in the cradle of supreme excellence when you evoke upon me a smile.
It resides in the beautiful calm in her eyes
that quiets my raging storm going wild
It paralyzes all my trust issues that I harbored deep inside
when her essence is poured upon me
She heats my inferno of loving just one woman
that was subsided up to a thousand degrees
She has commandeered all my past pains and fears
so I can love her with all of me
And the love making that we make will bring angelic beings to joyful tears.
She is here
my soul cries when she's near
for that she claimed it like the earth claims it hemispheres
My endearment for her goes far beyond loving with the love of a mere
mortal's heart
My love runs as deep as the Red Sea
every kiss and caress of hers is like a work of art
I would love to embark on an everlasting journey of loving her
for the very first time every time I wake up like the movie Groundhog Day.
And all I have to say…….
it is her that levels me in just one kiss
It is what she cradles between her thighs that is a picture portrait of bliss
It is her love that soars me above that I will forever miss
 if it's not in my line of sight
I will love with all thee above
using all my emotional might

THE AFTER GLOW

I can feel the calming of the racing of her heart
The crisp breeze of sensual sex is in the air from our erotic embark
Our conservative inhibition was torn apart
from ravishing our desires where temptation starts
The quickening of her sexual reactions and nature
Absorbs my essence whole
spitting out my inner player
Ripping the very fabric of my non-caking layers of issues
Our simultaneous climb was off the charts leaving intimacy the only thing
on the menu
I could continue to enclose her beautiful groves until the rapture arrives
Until my last breath fades
I will always yearn to be inside of her presence
In the future and present
I ache to cake with the core of her effervescence
For I'm captivated and stimulated by the vulnerable rhythms in her heart
 Baring to me in part the nakedness of her soul
A soothing confession easing my mental in the midst of our after glow
I cradle her in her vulnerability while our love of nectar is laced across our
lips and torsos
Fantasizing intuitively about us tasting the heavens
taking pleasure as far as it humanly can go
I feel as a whole that we will hit a higher plain of sweetness by resting in
each other's arms
Embracing her with my charms
as her soul is sweetly whispering to mines
We enjoy our down time from Kama Sutra-ing with bliss
But our embrace caking and kiss are as potent as our physical enlist
My spirit man will be more then remiss to have never indulged the
tranquility of you
A power that can devour any past pains
bringing serenity and simplicity through and through
From her nexus I will never become unglued
For she is the afterward connection that I've been searching for my entire
life

HER PROMISED LAND

Your essence is my Earth
Growing within me an addiction that can't be described in mere words
Your angelic voice is like a healing herb
that I slowly prescribe to my hungering soul
I'm at your complete control
when I'm in the lays of your beautiful land
For you are the stealth in my stride
that helps me thrive to stand like a man
Your promise land promises me a plan
To never feel emotional hunger or strife ever again
To find my immortal soul partner much
much more than just a girlfriend
Your aura ascends from the Almighty's hands to bless me with heaven on earth
Your birth was God's evidence to me that my life was worth living a thousand times over
The kiss of your sweet elegant scent makes me feel lucky as if I was a four leaf clover
When we are caught up and under in the grasp of our ecstasy
You oh so pleasure me
when I gaze in the midst of your Elysian Fields
Your wet dew cascades upon my lips and waist
a sweet taste that my desires would always find in it a great appeal
Your foundation is so surreal for it extends layers to my heart
Igniting a growth of life inwards of me
that I'm overwhelmed to be a part
You are the treasure of my heart
for that I will gladly bury in your holy ground
For your love always rises to the surface of me
I feel your vibe vibrating through me like surround sound
I will be more then down to pilgrimage your lands forever…
Forever more

THE RISE
(The Quickening of Love and Endearments)

YOUR WISH MY DESIRE

I am not a genie from a lamp
Nor am I a supernatural being
But I possess supernatural love when it comes to loving someone of your
standards.
I am not a genius
Nor am I a distinguished gentleman of caliber
But all I am after is your audience of acceptance
Choose to believe in me as I have already chosen to believe in your all.
I may not tell you what you want to hear all the time
But just know all the time I have your best interest and love at heart
Just know I dream the dreams that belong to you that stimulate you, and
bring you joy
I desire the wishes
 and the pleasant blessings that you request while gazing at a shooting star
I live for your happiness for it always recycles back within me
I may not have money or power
or even a great influence over others
But I do have my heart
And in this heart flows love, loyalty, genuineness
And in continuance with truth
I know love can't pay the bills
But love, faith, and understanding coming from someone true can pay the
way to a happy life, my love
For me you just being my wife is a understatement
We being together forever is just the beginning
I want our love
Your wish and my desire
To inspire others after us on how to truly adore one another
Our desire and our joyful intents
In all our events should be archived in the greatest love stories of all time
I want our names to be affiliated with Romeo and Juliet
Martin and Coretta
Penelope and Ulysses and all the immortal loves that are forever whispered
in our universal plain of time
Others may think to love like this to be considered strange
Or even insane
But I think it's very much sane to love something worthy
that fills your life with glory keeping you happy and content
To have a woman who you can trust to love more than yourself
So I say unto you on this night
as I swear on my soul with all my emotional might

Your love is my love
Your wants is my immediate need
Your simple wish will be my lunging desire
until we are dust….
Until we are dust.

THE HEAVENS ARE YOU

My place of true peace resides in you
everything that you say and do fills my heart with rushes of joy
A first and last resting place for my lovesick soul
I would eagerly employ
I hear sweet celestial serenades in the sound of your voice when applied to
me gently
I see breathtaking sunrises in your eyes
 when you gaze upon mortal me
The face of your beauty is so unreal so please don't be revealed as an
mirage
The embrace and taste of your nectar of flesh
it's like sampling food of the God's
I give homage to the presence of your serenity that dwells deep in the
insides of you
The picture portrait of perfection that mirrors you through and through
You are everything that I would design in a Queen
for you marrows it bone through bone
Your sweet angelic nature is my comforter guaranteeing that my soul will
never be alone
Our graceful lovemaking intent is like witnessing the events of the first
creation of man
An overwhelming flow of your excellence capsizes me
so from here on I want you to understand
That I will love you for my whole forever
for that you are my perfect eternity…

MY ENDEARMENT

I inhale and exhale the sweet remnants of your fragrance
Laced across my left pillow
that dances around my senses ever so delicately
So elegantly I peacefully dream
After sailing soothingly through your exquisite steaming streams
Bringing sweet serenity to my subconscious slumber
The spell that you have me under
bewitches my emotions
Spellbound my primitive addictions
For I shall never invoke this kind of devotion to any other woman again
For you make my everything ascend
past the tips of the Rocky Mountains
As your presence makes my nature rise a thousand miles and counting
Your touch blazes me blistering blissfully as if I was binging on a fountain
from the Universe's Sun
For this love
For this endearment that I am experiencing
will never be overrun or undone
For my heart will forever overrun............
With the fondness of you my Love

I OBSESSIVELY SEE

I see my everything in just one gaze
My own new Mecca that the Lord has beautifully laid
Each pillar of your greatness puts my concise being in a euphoric haze
and I'm so amazed how your essence applies to me
Please be my Eve
Let my bedroom chambers be our garden of tease
and sensual pleasurable touch
for I never
I mean never in my heart and desires craved to misbehave this much
until my present shared the presence of you
until the rapture of my lonely heart eclipsed in the form of you
for you are my sweet sunshine that penetrates through my broken heart of
gloom
You are my perfect obsession
so here I stand here in Sting form making you this confession
Every breath you take
Every move you make
Every hunger that your nature precipitates
I will be watching you
Every ounce of my creative mental being will be fixated on images of you
to taste and infiltrate your wonderful wetness is all I ache to do
Day and night fiending for that moment when my arms are blessed to be
able to console you
I'm hoping and wishing for that day
and I pray with everything in me at night
When you surrender your all to me outright
like I already did for you....
When my eyes met your glance.

MY FOREVER

As I close my eyes, and think about my forever
My forever happiness
My endless peace and without a forceful thought I saw you
Your captive smile
Your shimmering eyes that ever so divinely blends with your visage
A bountiful feast for my eyes it is like Thanksgiving to me
A gateway to your nexus
I'm seeking passage
To love the most lovable I can only imagine
The message I received from my heart after I gazed upon your stunning
Grail is that you are my forever
My forever love
My forever life
My mortal heaven plus two hundred multiplied by eleven
With you I see the simple pleasures being an oasis of bliss
I see our first date and our first kiss
A walk across the river walk holding hands as the wind whisks
Enjoying being in the presence of your company ever so glad I enlisted
Because you are my universe
my Neptune
my Mars
My milky way that I love to lick, nibble, and chew on
and so on
I can just see you lying across the couch with me watching Love Jones or
maybe Brown Sugar, my Brown Sugar
as your head lays at one end
With the laying of your ankles ever so rubbing and pressing upon my
manhood
And as I rub across your feet
and the tips of your toes with my warm strong hands
Feeling like Jerry McGuire saying to you "you complete me"
I wanna make sweet love with you all-night long and make you breakfast in
bed in the morning
Or I'll settle for just making you breakfast and slow winding you all day.
I'm like an adolescent on your playground
I want to swing all day
Play in your sand box
Slide down your slide
and ride on your merry go round
You will always be the forefront of my desires

My love is at your disposal
I will always be calling to your moist crevasses
even when we are both old and gray
The love lust factor of you
The eternity in your sweet midst
I can live twenty lifetimes and I won't ever find an equal like this
My forever
my sweet forever
I don't see it any other way.

THANKFUL FOR HER

I'm Thankful.......
for the love you bestowed upon me
A sweetness for my lunging soul that caresses me ever so gently
Beautifully your eyes engage my devotion completely
all in just one glance
They are telling me that you will pay homage to our love fully to make our
connection enhance
For all I want is for our hearts to do in rhythm is dance
while our chests are pressed upon one another in a passionate act
To bridge our endearments that we love to experience
allowing our desires to react
I'm Thankful...........
for the tender pleasures of your kiss
The taste of our physical enlist
a bountiful feast for my aching hunger that stimulates me whole
For it is greatness that you carry and uphold
when you relate to my wants and needs
You always know how to bring out the best in me
And suppress the worst that within me lies
She sees in me so much promise
that others miss through their judgmental eyes
What I truly realize with everything inside me.......
That I'm blessed for you giving me the gift
Blessing me with true gift in my life
For that I'm grateful for every angle of my life that involves you
on this day I'm thankful........
That you are in my arms tonight
so I can enjoy the bounty of your all

IN FEAR OF YOU

I'm scared of you
everything that you say and do
beautifully infiltrates my emotional borders
Your order in the way you relate to me
 captivates me to the point where my soul is at a standstill
My eyes rationalize with everything that I have inside
trying to visually reveal.......
Are you real!
Can the Lord design something with pure perfection
that glorious in every direction to where it's like unreal
I'm scared of you my love...........
a woman's essence never hit me like a ton of bricks
until your sweet kiss brushed across my unworthy lips
until my manhood penetrated your aching wet bliss
For it is the aura of your womanhood that really shackles my soul
That's why I can't get control of loving you more then I love myself
My selfishness excused itself
and filled that blank shelf with loving you until eternity fades
To adore you is like adoring coloring like I was a child in the first grade
not being able to help loving you
and only you with all my being is the reason at times........
That I'm truly afraid
I'm afraid to love a goddess
With mere mortal limitations applying emotional to you
I'm petrified that one day I will make you cry
and forever I will never hear from you
I'm totally capsized just by one look in your eyes
that infiltrates me through and through
But if the truth would be told
With no restrictions to be uphold
I fear I'm not enough for you
I feel like I'm fighting to uphold an illusion
And that you're under a temporary delusion
that I can make you happy as much you bring heaven to me
Your endearment is an unforgettable experience
 that tingles all over the whole of me
I'm scared of you my child ....
For I never loved anyone this much ever in my life
You as a whole
Influence my heart and soul

Hungering for that day for you to be my wife
In this life I truly know
I will always fear that my love is unequal to how you love me

THE ICING
**(Just Desserts
Of Love Layers)**

WELCOME

Welcome
You have penetrated my emotional barriers
healed my massive wounds in my most vulnerable areas
Blessed my presence with crisp completeness
While soothing me of my intimacy terrors
from now that I'm convinced
with a feeling so intense
That no one can ever love me better than you
After all that I went through
you were unflinchingly true by being you
you always projected grace in your stride
While ushering me through my blues
My Love, welcome...........
For you have slain all my demons of doubts
decompressed my self-esteem issues
allowing the real me to come out
Mentor to me the meaning of making love
and what truly being loved is all about
I've opened my essence for your entry
For it is you that I can't do without
That's why I say this to you as I joyfully scream and shout
Welcome...........
To my heart
To my soul
To my last breath if your last gasp won't be able to uphold
Welcome to a man to his heart to his eyes you have genius-ly unfolded
How to mend
How to be with pure perfection, a caring lover and best friend
And the secret.......
the art..............
of how to love again
Baby welcome

FAITH AND VOWS

I have faith in you........

That you will adore me with no bounds
accept me for who I am
And improve the round of my circle of peace

I have faith that you will teach.....
Teach me the art of truly making love
by molding my emotions in pure love
while exorcising me of my demons of the past

Because I know for me you will always stead fast to my betterment
overlook my problems of the past
And look forward to the present of where my promise for me lies

For in your heart with pride you has claimed me as your future everything
for even I know that you will be the bearer of my ring
Laced in an emotional 'I do'
Layered in vows of being there in rich, poor, sickness and health
For I will always feel well and wealthy when I'm with you

I want to share my life and last name with you
For you are my twin soul
my reincarnated Eve whose aura of essence that is engraved upon my soul
that is imprinted within me for eternity
so we can love each other immortally
Through the plains of our time
for that faith and true devotion can bridge across the sands of time

And with Agape and time you..........
You can do anything

For I know you are my everything that graces my visage with overwhelming
smiles

For I've waited all my whole life for you

I have faith.......
That you are fated to me
As I'm destined to truly loving you

For I solely believe.........
That the Lord wouldn't deny my life of being one with you
For our hearts are as one......
Faithfully vowed to each other

RESURRECTION OF THE CAPE

Look up in the sky it's a bird
it's a plane
no it is you.............
I see you
I see in you, my love, the truth
the proof that you exist that was told to me like fairy tales in my youth
the damsel in distress that if I rescued I would find my own salvation
my old cape that I sentenced to incineration
for that I was tricked by villain vexing of my past
The ones who sought what little I had
And demanded upon me my everything
Those false identities reeked upon me anarchy
traumatizing me from leaping tall single bounds looking for you
shying away from my mission for that I thought kryptonite resided in all
feminine crews
But then there was you.....
that became my red sun
The Phoenix that raised my brunt cape from the ashes and became my hero
unsung
The one who gave me my powers back of trusting and loving a woman past
my scorned self
For that my methods that I manifested for searching for you, my love, was
wrong
I was taught to trust every woman as long as they looked helpless and
appeared like they can not carry on
Not instilling in me that some victims in a demise
Can be users in disguise who look to play on you
Used and abused with no happy ending or to be continuously frequented
my relationship sagas
Many nights I would pray to God
to never allow love to find my black ass again
To never feel with endearing emotions for any woman outside of my kin
but it was you my super friend
Who trained me to love again
leading by example
As my trust levels went animal
Calming my beast within
in the heart of my city's soul darkest hour
I found you ushering me out my bitter campaign
it was you who showed me how it feels to be rescued for a change
who eased my pains

From my battle of archenemies of my past
who performed C.P.R. on my soul
In one look removing my mask of strain
you are....
My Mary Jane
My Lois Lane
My Rachel Dawes
My supernatural lover that gave my heart pause
unthawed my heart so it could beat again
I would risk it all
Give up it all
for you on my own sword I would gladly fall
to adore you, forever, my vigilante love
For you are now the protector and keeper of my all
For when I'm flying high with you I know that I will never fall
You saved my heart that was broken, scattered and corrupted
that's why for you my love........
I'm picking my cape back up

STORM BEHIND HER EYES

Talk to me
Open your heart up and just confide in me
I see your storm within that you're trying to hide behind your eyes
a river of your raging emotions that you have bottled deep inside........
Your emotional abyss
I feel the withdrawal in your kiss
the fading decadence in our physical enlist
torments my calm like a splinter deep in my mind
Let it be a podium that your trust can find so your true heart can speak
I vow to have my ears on hustle
and have my reactions set to meek
Baby is it me?
Am I'm being emotionally responsible enough for all your desires, wants
and needs?
Does my embrace warm you physically and your gentle aura at night?
Does your wing, my beautiful swan, need to spread in the format of a hiatus
flight...... ?
I mean do you need space?
For I'll rather eject myself across the outer limits of space
before I jeopardize forever being away from your sweet embrace
Is it your own personal bubble you need to preserve and taste?
How do I give you grace from your hurricane that's leveling your calm and
peace?
Higher plateau of tranquility and simplicity
I'm willing to help you seek
let me relate to your troubles
for I vow to be subtle in your situation
Put your faith in us in the form of honest communication
but it all starts with you talking to me
It all starts with your soul opening up and speaking freely
Let your trust bridge you to me
To exorcise all the demons that haunt you now
your winds are wailing
your inward pain is chanting loud
Oh how I miss your natural smile that comforted me as a whole
Don't let silent actions take control
for I see your war raging
your storm rampaging
and your heart hesitating when its respond to me
For this situation crestfallen me deeply
For tonight I pray.......

I pray that the truth in our communications can find intimacy
I can feel and see your emotional everything
by reading in your eyes
where your gentle soul and sweet essence lays
Baby, I just want you my love to realize.......
that you can always talk to me.

A LETTER OF MY REGRET

My pride has made a fool of me
for anyone that knows us knows…
that you were the better part of me.
For I am an average man
But, my love, you always make me great
and with everything it takes, you always yearned to make me better
the flawlessness in you always unflawed the imperfection that lies within me
And the images of the future man that you thought I could really be
always left me in disbelief
for you were so sweet
and I was so arrogant
to the point where it was apparent that I didn't want to change or show you
the same range of emotion for you in my heart
for you adored me past the point of any entity feeling worshipped
Knowing deep in the depths of the back of my mind that I didn't deserve it
and now all I can do is sit here and absorb it
and absorb this whole scenario deep in my cerebral
at home in my land of the damned
With my whole world in upheaval saying "she's out of my life"
I let the past of unstable creatures
the present of physical meaningless lust
and the future of fear in failing to be a better man
mess up my present and future with you
Now all I can do is rehash the past
back when I was yours and you was my baby
at home alone going crazy
drowning in all my sorrows and caking with all my regrets
But with all due respect to myself, my love
You can do better than me
It took everything in me to think like a man to say that to you
It took everything within me to understand that all birds aren't meant to be
caged
Especially a swan like you with sparrow like beauty that dazzles everyone in
the sky and clouds
Now if I'm further allowed
even though I ache for you every day
in every single physical and emotional way….
My true heart wants you to be happy
My true humanity for the peace that I seek ahead of me yearns for you to
find true intimacy
even if it's in the arms of my sworn enemy

because you deserve your happy ever after at any cost
and out of everything that I have lost in my trying life
I will always regret losing you
For my tragic loss shall one day be
that worthy man immortal gain
that's why I will always forever feel this exquisite pain
and these regretful chains that shackle my heart
that feels like someone taking a rusty knife and ripping my essence and my
soul apart
My pride has made a fool of me
because anybody that knows us knows....
that you were the better part of me
Be happy, my love.

REKINDLING HER MEMORY

I remember you
I so blissfully remember you
the warmth that generates from you when we bond hands
the way you would glide when you slow danced with me
As I indulge in your aura while you're entwined in the grips of my arms
my heart feels like a perfect beat
when yours are pressed next to mines
my cares of my world just recline to the will of you giving me bliss
And when we kiss.........
Its like the fourth of July for my longing soul
For you are the sole........
The sole reason why my lips are occupied by plenty of smiles
the sole reason why I feel like a lovesick child
 When you address me with your presence
Just living in the essence of your memories
of when you were with me
 pacifies me from my weary days
But in so many ways.........
When you're not here you still complete me
For all I have to do is reminisce about you and me
and I will feel whole while styling a massive smile
For within my cerebral I would search a million brain cell miles
to retrieve and relive in the moments of being with you
For you are my Solaris
my perfect planet paradise that wills me perfection
in so many insertions of you
Your touch tantalizes my senses
in any event I enjoy the mental playback of the all of you
For all I desire to do is remember you
Rekindling when you was loving me

COME BACK TO ME

You are the one that got away
the one I should have wifed
and shared the rest of my life with back in our day
In my arms is where you should have forever laid
until the last of our elderly breath faded away
until the benediction of the worlds' end is in play
until the essence of our love has no more love to manifest or give away
For you have displayed true love to me
you showed me that love can survive under straining emotional degrees
Back then I was emotionally blind
because your love and devotion I could not see
so to you right now I make this plea
let my senses know the warmth of your touch again
let my taste buds sweetly tingle from experiencing your delectable flesh
within
Let our embrace rekindle our intimate enchantments
so our love can beautifully mend
let our soul bond
as our emotions explode like a bomb
and amore past where mere human obsession end
Let me once again
Please let me once again..........
love the greatness of you
For your love made the greatness that once resided in me
Please..........
let us love each other again

BONUS
A Dedication to Eve

HER REHAB

All I wanna to do is just heal her
Find all her broken pieces and gently rebuild her
Embrace upon her my caress that's engaged so tender
sprinkle her heart and soul with serenity
For my essence to her I will gladly surrender
Agape to her I will unlimitedly render
Keep her emotions out of her bad memories danger
Pacify her anger with the dedication of sweetness and meekness
Be the chemo to her broken hearted cancer
I just so wanna beautifully enhance her
Make her whole beyond anger's hold
Give her that moment of clarity
Take back what her past abusers maliciously stole
Let my arms be the one that her insecurities let console
Prove to her inner demons that I will forever be around
Stimulate her inner Queen
Help her find her self love along with her crown
With no boundaries barred I believe I can achieve this
Give evidence to her deep- seated doubts that true love not just
dysfunctional love does exist
And all that I ask for all of this............
Is to let me try.........
To love her
Let my deep seed endearments console her
Let every angle of my physical and emotional being pledge allegiance to her
for all I desire to do is be a healer to her
Give her intimate rehab
nurture her through her times when they're bad
and prove to her heart
and as a whole...............
that I will always be there for her
Please............
Let me rehab the all of her

YOU ARE ALL WOMAN TO ME

Let my arms console you
let my soul hold you my tormented soul
For I will not let harm come to you
May my kiss cascade your hands and wrist
Leading to your broken heart
your poor broken heart
that your last love vigorously ripped apart
I don't know if I can save you
But I can offer you my love a kind hand
A warrior that will battle for you to the end
Honor you and take a stand
A person that will truly love and adore you as a farmer adores his land
I will carry you with respect and pride
 With everything inside
 The true essence of a man
I would be your best friend or boyfriend in whatever order you need me to
be
in a loving act
I will never hold back
Giving me to you completely
I could never make you forget how your pain of the past affected you
But I can make you realize
right before your eyes that functional love does deserve you
A happy ending that is unbending is truly worthy of you
No matter how deep was your strain
And the love you loved in vain
Or anything that you went through
I will hold you in the middle of the night
when you wake up in fright
From your nightmares that visit you
I don't know if I can save you my love
but I know that I will never lie to you
I know that I can be your rock
When your tears won't stop
And someone that you can confide into
I will believe in you
For I see in you greatness that's covered under all your abused scars
I see you through your walls of distrust
That your past lovers helped build up
A beautiful moon among the stars
You are all woman

As far as my eyes can see
your past boyfriend that wasn't able to see
doesn't qualify as a man to me
if I was ever to hurt you while you're with me
Please charge it to my head and not to my heart
because for in this heart my rhythms only beat for you
until the blood that flows to it stops
I don't know if I can save you my dear love
But I will promise you that I would for always love and cherish you
For you are all woman to me

INSTRUCTIONS FOR A QUEEN

If to her you must lie........
Lie in her arms in the calm of her lonely nights
If you ever make her cry
Make it be cries of delight from you giving her joy in an abundant mass
And if you must ever deny her
Deny her of the characteristics of her abusers of her past
Let your every action prove that you are not him
let that be your most important task
And if you must neglect her
Neglect her mistakes of her past that at times rear up in your present
And If you must indulge in a drink around her
Drink of the sweet scent of her effervescence let your being be intoxicated
by her soul
If you must fail her
Fail her in breaking her heart or her self esteem as a whole.
Let the best of your intentions be in full control for it is gentleness upon
her you want to bestow
If you must put your hands on her
Put your hands on her with open palms baptized in warm soothing oil
Make every tense nerve ending on her body feel spoiled
Gently massage her every open pore ranging from her shoulder to her wrist
Along with slight tender chops down the small of her back, making all her
physical senses feel bliss
And after her touch session seal her sedated state with a soft lingering kiss
If you must make her feel weak
Make her weak from multiple orgasmic peaks
Make all of her sexual hunger embrace satisfaction that feels so sweet
If you ever have to come between her
Come between her passionately in the midst of a intimate enlist
Wind and grind with her in a heavenly sequence for filling her every lustful
wish
Make her your favorite full course dish while being a member of the clean
plate club
Make every angle of her entire being feel ecstasy and love
If you must steal from her.......
Steal from her cares so her happiness can always stay in flight
And if you ever leave her.........
Leave her in sheer delight from all your acts of pleasure and show of
endearments
Never let her emotions be your own emotional experiment
Keep her surrounded in a loving and supporting environment

And if you must cheat on her..........
Cheat her of all her troubles and cares; let her vexes be celibate
Wrapping her tight with peace, tranquility, laced in elegance and sweet joy
For these are some of the acts that I will forever employ on a lady of true caliber
For to have a true woman of great valor........
Is my definition of heaven on Earth

HER SACRIFICE

She kisses the side of my face as she wakes
Brush the sides of my loc's as she leaves
Seeing a greatness within me that at times I don't believe
To achieve a smile upon my visage
 to her it's her mission accomplished
Putting away all the cares of her world she's so beautiful
So amazingly kind and honest
She promises with a full heart to adore
And vows with everything not to injure me emotionally
As I wish that I can also vow to her
But mental flashbacks of my relationship trauma won't let me
When she touched my life
That was cold as ice
That will provoke an Eskimo to blurs
To give the heat of her rapture and my salvation
Is all that she was after, makes me want to unthaw for her
She says she is just a world that spins on the axle of my acceptance
Saying that the sins of my past to her was truly irrelevant
But what was self-evident to me is that she was the greatness that I need
The light tower in my darkest hour
To illuminate me from the self-hatred of me
Her everything she offered to unworthy me just to be the savior of me
So one day that I will embrace love's trust
But my inner demons speak to me
It's not a possibility
deep down in me I know
if I was to trust her intentions
and touch all my past baggage will unload
and I will be able to uphold love in my heart once again
For that she is my intimate friend....
That sees in me much more

NO MATCH

How does it feel to have the ability to change a frown into a smile?
To be heard without speaking
To enrich a man's imagination just by the very thought of you
To be supremely intoxicating with passion and femininity
To make completely the strongest of strong man putty in your hand
A vision of pure beauty tempered with greatness and excellence
I'm no match for the measure of woman you are
You hold the greatest of great in your enthralled,
tranquility, glory and blissful simplicity resides in your palm
Perfection seeps from every angle of you
you are desire's desire.
The Fahrenheit to the sun that shines over my being
you have the truth and a loving heart wrapped in your sweet skin
the overlay of a power that can shift disappears into bliss
and depression into sheer delight
I'm no match for the measure of women you are
The silhouette of you shimmers down a tenderness equaled by no one
Your touch sings sweet songs of the Ancient's
Back when pyramids were being formed and when Pharaohs ruled my
Queen Sheba
Just gazing upon your stunning gaze makes me feel the sand across my feet
The architect of my climactic climaxes
And the sweetness of my sweetest dreams that makes me yearn for a coma
For me it's like a holiday every time I make love to you
I'm no match for the measure of woman you are
I'm NO MATCH for the measure of woman you are.

HOW TO LOVE YOUR EVE

Treat her like your day and night
Be her light when she's in the abyss of her calamity
Show her with no doubt that you're striving to be the best man that you can
be
When you're together relate to her gently as a poet relating to a beautiful
verse
Look deeply into her eyes like she's the last woman on the planet earth
Wrap her vessel tight when in the midst of the winter days
Hold her even tighter when you're in the heat of your summer days
Give her room for her dreams to graze
But always display that love is not far behind
When embracing your lips with hers, sample them slowly like sipping a fine
exquisite wine
When making love to her treat her frame likes a work of art
Stroke her canvas in slow stroking rhythms
While evoking within her your soul and heart
Cradle her in the vulnerability of her afterglow
Let your cake be limitless
but feed it to her in a natural flow
Love her and respect her
and never hold a meaningless grudge
Listen to all the problems your woman has but at the same time never be
her judge
Show her in your reactions
even in the world's distractions that she's the only one you adore and love
Treasure her essence
and put no other woman above her
Believe in your Eve and there will be no end for the show of her love
For that nothing could ever be above the high that you feel when your Eve
truly loves you

A DAUGHTER'S PROMISE TO DADDY

My beautiful soon to be Queens
I see so much greatness that awaits you
let my wisdom lace your self esteem and mental
let my tutelage right now embrace you
and please promise me.......
That you live and love in your life not like me
I know when you look upon me
You see a man that loves and adores you with his soul completely
But some things in my life.....
Your father has failed miserably
Daddy's little girls please let your listening attention indulge me
First of all.....
don't be scared of living
feast upon every moment by moment like a family dining at its first
Thanksgiving
Live for your today, but always plan for your tomorrows
Rebel against self- loathing depression
for it will make you feel like your time is borrowed
never indulge in its symphony of its destructive sorrow
for it will dance you into an early grave
Make others honor your worth and learn from the mistakes that you have
made
Treat other how you want to be treated
make sure they treat you well as well or from your inner circle they should
be deleted
Never be someone's willing victim or never ever their abuser
or their tormentor or false accuser
Let truthfulness run through you freely
Be genuine in all your actions
 and let your intentions react honorably
and when that day comes that you choose to seek love..............
Don't let it be a Nigga like me
Or more like the person that I allowed myself in the past to be
Find someone who blends with your all like tides rippling in the calm of the
sea
Make sure he amours and adores you completely
And if he ever ceases to love you, my child
remember there's always more fish in the sea
That will see the beauty in you that Daddy sees back to when I held your in
my arms

Never give your body to a man who depends and lives on his arrogance and
charms
Never disarm your womanhood for the insecurities of any man
Always take a firm stand when it comes to your intimate expectations
and if he is worthy of you my darling love him like God loves all his
creations
Allow him to be your King
but never your dictator
and you should be his Queen
and never his aggravator
Be his slice of heaven and allow him to be your elixir of bliss
Love him for who he is, not because he made a superficial check list
Let communication and endearing intent
Illuminate you both in your day to day
For these are some of my life lessons that I learned from my wayward ways
for when your time comes, my Daughters, hopefully these lessons will apply
to you
So your future won't ever mimic my past
and be afraid to love because you was someone's fool
So my little Princess of my bloodline
I say unto you
please promise me.......
That you will live and love in your life to the full
A lot better than me

ACKNOWLEDGMENTS

Writing this book has been a labor of love. First and foremost, I give honor to God for blessing me with the gift of life and for all the loved ones that He's allowed to be in my life who have shown me love and given me strength.

I want to thank LaShaun Pheonix Kotaran for being my ambassador through the realms of poetry. Without her my poetic endeavors would not be possible. I want to thank Dimonique Boyd for her encouragement, guidance and her help in making this book possible.

I want to thank Nandi at Nandi's Knowledge Café for supplying a poetic haven of my own.

I give thanks to my Detroit poetry community as a whole for giving me love with my poetry and constructive criticism when I needed it.

I want to thank my children for being the beacon of light in my life. I want to thank my family for blessing me with the best support system known to man.

Last but not least, I want to give honor to my editor for believing in me through thick and thin even when others didn't. Without her my muse would not be what it is today. Thank you from the bottom of my heart.

Made in the USA
Charleston, SC
03 October 2012